THE PURPOSE OF THE PRIESTHOOD:

A MESSAGE FROM CHRIST

Written and illustrated
by
Elizabeth Wang

A selection of other works by Elizabeth Wang also published by Radiant Light:

Teachings-in-Prayer Volume One: Spiritual Training.
Teachings-in-Prayer Volume Two: Spiritual Nourishment.
Teachings-in-Prayer Volume Three: Spiritual Work.
Teachings-in-Prayer Volume Four: Spiritual Life.
Teachings-in-Prayer Volume Five: Spiritual Peace.
"My Priests are Sacred."
How to Pray (Part One: Foundations)
How to Pray, Part Two: Liturgy and Morals.
Falling in Love: A Spiritual Autobiography.
Radiant Light: How the Work Began.
"Speak about Hope."
"Speak about Holiness."
What is Jesus like?
What is Mary like?
The Majesty of the Mass.
The Beauty of the Rosary.
The Glory of the Holy Trinity.
The Wonder of the Christian Story.
The Mass Through the Eyes of Christ.
Prayer Postcards: Hope and encouragement.
Rosary Postcards.
An Invitation from Christ: prayer card.
A Message from the Father: prayer card.
For Prisoners and those in Darkness: prayer card.
A Prayer to Jesus in His Suffering: prayer card.
Jesus Speaks about the Holy Eucharist: prayer card.
Our Lady of Harpenden: blank prayer card.
The Holy Sacrifice of the Mass: Mass Poster.
A3 Posters (various)
Radiant Light Conference Video 1999.
Radiant Light Conference Video 2000.
The Christian Story Video.

For information about how to order Radiant Light products please visit **www.radiantlight.org.uk** or write to request a catalogue from:
**Radiant Light, 25 Rothamsted Avenue,
Harpenden, Herts, AL5 2DN, U.K.**

THE PURPOSE OF THE PRIESTHOOD:

A MESSAGE FROM CHRIST

Written and Illustrated by
Elizabeth Wang

This book is published by **Radiant Light**
25 Rothamsted Avenue
Harpenden, Herts., AL5 2DN, U.K.

First published March 2005

'C.C.C.' refers to the *'Catechism of the Catholic Church'*,
Geoffrey Chapman, London 1994, copyright © 1994
Geoffrey Chapman - Libreria Editrice Vaticana

Scripture quotations have been taken from The Jerusalem Bible
published and copyright © 1966, 1967 and 1968
by Darton, Longman and Todd Ltd
and Doubleday & Co. Inc.

Text and illustrations by Elizabeth Wang
Text and illustrations copyright © Radiant Light 2005

Front cover design: painting by Elizabeth Wang
"Christ our Intercessor"
W/COL: 0811

ISBN 1-902960-43-2

A passage from the Second Letter of St. Paul to Timothy.

'Before God and before Christ Jesus who is to be judge of the living and the dead, I put this duty to you, in the name of his Appearing and of his kingdom: proclaim the message and, welcome or unwelcome, insist on it. Refute falsehood, correct error, call to obedience - but do all with patience and with the intention of teaching. The time is sure to come when, far from being content with sound teaching, people will be avid for the latest novelty and collect themselves a whole series of teachers according to their own tastes; and then, instead of listening to the truth, they will turn to myths. Be careful always to choose the right course; be brave under trials; make the preaching of the Good News your life's work, in thoroughgoing service.' (2 Tim 4:1-5)

CONTENTS

Section	Page No.
A list of illustrations	2
An introduction	3
The light of truth	6
A ladder to Heaven	9
Questions to ponder	13
Twelve spiritual dangers	15
1. Infrequent prayer	15
2. Refusing to accept unexpected suffering	16
3. Self-centred instead of God-centred prayer	17
4. Lack of full attention in prayer	18
5. Clinging to our sins	19
6. Over-emphasis on self-esteem	20
7. Timidity	22
8. Poor instruction	24
9. Disregard for the Magisterium	26
10. Resentment	28
11. Incessant grumbling	29
12. Lack of reverence	30
Ready for Heaven?	35
A Special Message	37
Conclusion	39

LIST OF ILLUSTRATIONS

Page No.

Cover: Christ our Intercessor

1. A dark world 41
2. The ladder to Heaven 43
3. With bleeding hands 45
4. Waiting to greet us 47
5. The Christ-child 49
6. Preaching to 'wounded' souls 51
7. A warning is an act of charity 53
8. Out of communion 55
9. The Institution of the Eucharist 57
10. Christ our Intercessor 59

INTRODUCTION

A difficult decision

In September 2004 an unexpected invitation was held out to me in a letter from a Catholic priest. He had read some of my books about the spiritual life. Now he was wondering if I was willing to give a talk to the group of priest-friends with whom he spends a week on retreat each year.

Whenever I am faced with a decision I turn to the Lord for help, in prayer; so I did so once again. My difficulty was that, as a lay-woman and a convert, I have been happier to receive advice from priests than to give it. But the Lord solved my problem.

First, Christ asked me not to be afraid to share, with priests, those teachings which He has already given me for the Clergy. I have already published many of those 'teachings' in 'Radiant Light' books and pamphlets. Secondly, He showed me in prayer some new images, with detailed descriptions of His purpose in doing so. He invited me to share His words and images with priests on this retreat, and thus to give a reminder of the purpose of the Priesthood. He also invited me to print these in a booklet for other priests to read. So this booklet is Christ's idea, not my own. Only to please Him have I written and published this enlarged account of what I said at All Saints Pastoral Centre, London Colney, on 28 October 2004.

It's because I first offered 'The purpose of the Priesthood' as a talk and not as a written article that I use direct speech, addressing 'you priests,' and speaking about 'us the laity.'

Personal responses

This booklet is not a complete theology of the Priesthood. Nor does it contain anything new. It is simply a reminder of some aspects of the Priesthood which are especially relevant today and which the Lord has asked me to mention. If it seems to present a limited view of the spiritual life, with much about the life of an individual Christian, but far less about his relationship with the Church, this is deliberate. Christ has asked me to speak here about our personal response to the Gospel, and about the importance of perseverance.

No soul who has not repented can 'smuggle' himself into Heaven, hidden in a crowd of sincere, loving believers. One at a time, we shall die, and meet God, and greet Him with gladness and awe, or horror. That is why we need actively to prepare for Heaven, or risk the loss of God. That is the central motif in this message for priests. There are other books and other illustrations of mine which deal with equally important aspects of the spiritual life, and with Christ and His Church, the sacraments, the Communion of Saints, and our loving concern for our neighbour.

Before I begin, I must say how very indebted I am to the priests I've met since I was received into full communion with the Catholic Church, nearly forty years ago. It seems to me that you have all surrendered your lives to Christ with magnificent courage and generosity. Nothing of what follows, therefore, should be seen as personal criticism. I simply repeat some loving reminders from the Lord about a number of wide-spread problems in the Church. Christ has told me that you can help to solve them by offering even braver and fuller explanations of the Faith, both in your preaching and in your one-to-one pastoral encounters.

One Pope quotes another

The Holy Father, Pope John Paul II, has recently published a book about his own ministry. In *'Rise, Let Us Be On Our Way'* he quotes a few words of Pope St. Gregory the Great who once bewailed, in the following words, the lack of sound preaching in his era: *'... the people entrusted to our care are abandoning God and we remain silent.'* Christ has shown me that the same thing is happening in large parts of the Church today. This is why Christ has offered a warning, through me, that many people today, who claim to be 'practising Catholics,' quite deliberately disobey God's Commandments, and even urge others to be disobedient.

It is true that there is more to 'life in Christ' than keeping rules and regulations, as countless spiritual writers have told us in recent times. Yet Christ wants you to lead us towards holiness and salvation. He wants to be able to count on every priest *'for both expounding the sound doctrine and refuting those who argue against it'* (Titus 1:9).

Some Catholics today have few reminders about the need to avoid sin as well as to do good. Some are fervent in working to help the poor, or to build peace, yet see no harm in their own co-habitation with a partner, or civil 're-marriage' outside the Church, or pro-abortion stance, or contraceptive use, or neglect of prayer and the sacraments.

On the one hand, it is not right for us to judge one another. We cannot know what goes on in other souls, and what sort of relationship they have with God. Christ once said of a woman *'who had a bad name in the town'* (Lk 7:37) that *'her many sins must have been forgiven her, or she would not have shown such great love'* (Lk 7:47). He was warning Simon, the host, not to despise or ignore anyone, no matter what he might have heard from other people. On the other hand, the realisation that we must not condemn others, and that we are all sinners, must not cause Catholics in responsible posts today to refrain from teaching the truth about right and wrong behaviour.

Truthful teachings

Many Catholics who live in objectively-sinful relationships, or who defend immoral practises, have never been told, with both clarity and charity, that the teachings of the Church are true. They have never been told that we can find peace-of-soul amidst our difficulties if we will listen to the Catholic Church, and with God's help keep the Commandments.

The plain truth is that priests who are willing to serve Christ in simplicity and trust, and to speak about our need of penance and purification, can help to save those of us who are tempted to follow the broad road away from God.

Through your preaching, you can open our eyes to one of the pivotal truths about God, and about us who are immensely precious to Him. It is that God allows us, by our freely-made decisions, to move towards Him (with His help) in repentance and hope, or to turn away, rejecting His love and forgiveness.

By our own choices, we shall one day arrive in Heaven, by His grace, or in Hell - though a journey to Heaven might be preceded by Purgatory. The important point is that Christ is asking you priests to be truthful as well as kind to the people in your care so that we are *'not ruled by human passions but only by the will of God'* (1 Pet 4:2). He urges you not to be afraid to say, when necessary: *'you must repent and turn to God, so that your sins may be wiped out'* (Acts 3:19).

He also asks you to *'be an example that the whole flock can follow. When the chief shepherd appears, you will be given the crown of unfading glory'* (1 Pet 5:4).

THE LIGHT OF TRUTH

Demands on your time

It can be difficult for you priests to remain 'focused' today, amidst all the demands upon your time. There are very many pressures upon you to campaign for one thing, or become involved in another, as well as to fulfil your ordinary duties. And Christ looks on with tremendous love, as you try to discern His Will, and to make wise decisions about your everyday lives. Yet He now invites you to reflect once again on the words uttered during each Ordination Mass, when a Bishop proclaims that the task of a new priest is **'to offer sacrifice and to sanctify the Christian people.'**

The Holy Sacrifice of the Mass, which you offer daily, is illustrated on the front cover of this booklet, as well as near the end. This painting (*10: Christ our Intercessor*) serves as a reminder that Christ the God-man, now risen from the dead, is substantially Present in the Blessed Sacrament. In our sanctuary, as in Heaven, He perpetually intercedes for us. And if you'll remember how kind He is, and how powerful, you will not worry about your weaknesses. He wants you to believe that by apparently ordinary or insignificant words and actions in your daily lives, you can cause the blazing light of truth to shine in the minds of those you serve - whether or not you are aware of such moments of grace.

You might ask: What are the principal truths that the Lord wants us to show out, in this age? He wants you to realise that a lot of people in the Church rightly share truths about justice, and about poverty, and war and arms-dealing; but far fewer speak about Heaven and Hell, about sin and salvation, and about saving souls - which are the important but neglected truths that the Lord wants me to put before you, today.

If you are courageous in your preaching, and patient and faithful in your everyday work as priests, you can bring about great changes in the lives of people around you, and in the lives of their friends or relations. This is true even if you aren't at present aware of your impact. That's why the Lord is asking you to look again at what you think, say and do, as you go about your task of sanctifying the Christian people.

Back to basics

Christ wants you to work to make us holy. A really holy person is someone who has become Christ-like. In the end, a holy person has avoided Hell, and gained Heaven through Christ. In persevering to that point he or she has loved and served God with wholehearted love and obedience, and has loved and served his or her neighbour, for God's sake. And since the Lord Who chose you for the Priesthood has asked you to help others to achieve perfect and eternal union with God, He invites you to look carefully at the ways in which you help us. He asks you to go 'back to basics.'

The essence of your task is to reconcile sinners with God, whether these 'sinners' in need of God's grace be the unbaptised, or Catholics or other Christians. Yet Christ has told me that many of you are afraid to speak the truth about sin and salvation in case you 'drive people away.' That is why He has given me some images to share. They will remind you of the vast 'gulf' there is between the sinfulness of human beings, and the blazing holiness of the Godhead. They might remind you, therefore, of the tremendous importance of your priestly work.

The need for repentance

Christ wants you to preach the Gospel that He preached in His earthly life: about God the Father's love for us all, certainly, but also about the need for repentance. He asks you, today, to repent of your own failings, if you have ever preached a ***'new gospel, different from the one you have already accepted'*** (2 Cor 11:4). And He asks you to repeat to everyone in your care the message He preached as He set out on His own earthly ministry: ***'Repent, for the kingdom of heaven is close at hand'*** (Mt 4:17).

A LADDER TO HEAVEN

A sinful world

The first image given to me in prayer, by Christ, to share with you, is near the end of this booklet. *1. 'A dark world'* shows the globe of the earth, half-hidden in shadow, in the darkness of space. In the top right-hand corner of the painting you can see a few bright orange flames which indicate the existence, far 'above' our world, of the fiery glory of Heaven. Neither earth nor Heaven, however, should be seen as the focal point of this image. The Lord is asking us all to look at the gap between Heaven and earth: at the gulf between Heaven's purity and beauty, and earth's sinfulness and gloom. Despite the fact that God created the world, and saw it as 'good', something went terribly wrong. Humanity became trapped in sin and selfishness, and cut off from the holiness and salvation which God was holding out to us.

As you know, the gap between Heaven and earth was eventually bridged by God Himself, in the Person of His Son, Jesus Christ - through the action of the Holy Spirit - when God became man, to deliver us from our sins. Christ 'descended' from Heaven, at His Incarnation. He left behind His glory, to rescue us from darkness; and something of His saving work is shown out in another image given to me especially for priests, which is the second of the set of ten images I've placed at the end of this booklet.

The life of grace

In this picture (*2: 'The ladder to Heaven'*) we can see the earth again - though the darkness is not as dark as before. Everything has changed, since the Incarnation. That amazing event has occurred. Almighty God has decided to come down amongst us, in the Person of His Son, to die for our sins, and to make possible a new way of life for human beings. This is why you can see in this picture a large mountain which was not visible before. The mountain has a flat top, which is brilliantly lit - as if reflecting the light of Heaven. That bright, flat area represents the life of grace, and the 'height' to which we are brought through our Baptism. It also represents the radiance of a soul in a state of grace: someone no longer 'lost' in the darkness of sin.

From within that life of grace there has emerged a means of reaching the glory of Heaven. A narrow rope ladder bridges the gulf from the bottom left to the top right of the painting; and the ladder represents perseverance. It is not necessarily 'enough' for us to be baptised. Many of us survive childhood, and in passing through adult life we are tempted or even corrupted by evil influences around us. We need to repent, to grow more Christ-like day by day, and to remain faithful until we die.

Christ asks us to remember that we cannot persevere without His help. If we really love Christ, it is inevitable that we shall meet temptations and trials. Some will be so fierce that it will seem as if we are trying to cling on to a rope ladder in a force-ten gale.

There are a hundred things in our own nature that can pull us off course. There are people around us who would like to wreck our faith. The evil one has all sorts of ways of dragging us away from God's service. So it's a long way to Heaven, in one sense, if we want to persevere. Yet we are called to an amazing destiny. The thought of being able to share in the life of the Holy Trinity for all Eternity, in a known way, is mind-boggling. We should surely be able to explain it with enough enthusiasm and fervour so as to ignite at least a little interest in the minds and hearts of other people.

Union, or alienation

We all need to tell people that we don't just drift into Heaven. There is work to be done if we want to be sure of arriving there, by God's grace. So what Christ asks of you, who are profoundly involved in the care of our souls, is that you fervently steer us in the right direction, and, whilst encouraging us to trust in God, remind us of the dangers around us. Each of us can choose whether to keep climbing that 'ladder' to Glory or to fall back into the darkness of worldly life. If we remain in this darkness we unavoidably follow the wide and spacious **'road that leads to perdition'** (Mt 7:13).

There is no 'third way' or middle road. There is only union with God, at the end of our lives, or alienation from Him. This is the message of Christ our God, and of the Apostles whose passionate words of encouragement and warning fill the pages of the New Testament. And this is why Christ has given a special task to you, His priests, and offers you in this booklet a reminder of its importance.

Other Christs

Each of you priests is to be another Christ. Christ asks you to preach and to offer sacrifice with tremendous conviction and fervour. You are being asked to bridge that gulf between the darkness of earthly life and the glory of Heaven. Each of you is invited to act in Christ's name, and to do all you can to bring us closer to Heaven. Christ has shown me that you can do this in three particular ways. You know these already; but Christ wants you to hear these reminders.

He has chosen and prepared you, so that (A) *you point out the way to Heaven*, (B) *you prepare us for Heaven,* and (C) *you 'touch' Heaven every day in the Mass.*

(A) *You point out the way to Heaven* by preaching the truth about Christ: about the great 'descent' He made out of love for us; about how He sacrificed His life, without complaint, to save us; about the New Covenant He made between God and man, a Covenant which He sealed with His own blood, poured out for our sakes on the Cross; and about His heartfelt plea to us that we repent of our sins, and change our lives. You can remind us that through the sacraments we share Christ's Divine life; and thus, in our weakness, we have the power to live in purity and peace, in the service of God and neighbour.

(B) *You prepare us for Heaven* by celebrating the sacraments with us and for us. Through the sacraments the graces of Christ, won for us by His death and Resurrection, are lavished upon those of us who are willing to receive them. We need to be reminded that we need the sacraments, if we are sincere in wanting to become **'as pure as Christ'** (1 Jn 3:3). Christ has told me that anyone who wishes to examine his own state of readiness for Heaven can ask 'Am I ready to see Christ and Our Lady face to face, without shame?' You priests can ask that question of yourselves, and encourage us, too, to think about it. And if any of us answers 'not yet', about our readiness to look upon our Saviour, the questions must follow: What we are doing, in preparation for that meeting? When are we going to make up our minds?

(C) *You 'touch' Heaven every day in the Mass*; and you can inform the people you serve that the Mass is more than a memorial meal. At every Mass we are united with the whole Church of earth and Heaven and Purgatory, in the presence of the holy Angels. Christ our God is made Really Present at the Consecration. He Who has just reached out to teach and console us in the words of Holy Scripture is now amongst us, praying to the Father, in the Spirit, on behalf of the living and the departed. And Christ's sacrificial prayer is so powerful that it leaps across the dark gulf which separates Heaven and earth. We 'touch' Heaven at every Mass, in and through Christ, and through your sacred ministry; and Christ's prayers are always heard and answered. These are truths so glorious and astounding that we should be sharing them at every opportunity.

QUESTIONS TO PONDER

Worthy of Heaven?

Christ knows very well that you already know these things. Many of you have laboured for years, in great hardship, to preach and to offer sacrifice for the glory of God and the good of souls. Yet Christ Who sees all your good works has some questions for you to ponder.

- Do you speak more about service to the community than about other equally-important things? How often do you speak about union with God? How often do you speak to your people about Heaven, as you preach, baptise, and offer the Holy Sacrifice? Do you ever mention Hell?

- Why do so many Catholics today imagine that if we are nice to people, and try not to hurt anyone, we shall drift into Heaven in the end, no matter what sort of lives we have led? Do you believe that their parents have failed to teach them, or their school-teachers, or the Clergy?

The narrow gate

Christ has shown me one of the reasons for the great drift away from faith by many Catholics today. Few have been told, by brave and truthful preachers, teachers or parents, that **'it is a narrow gate and a hard road that leads to life, and only a few find it.'** (Mt 7:14)

Perhaps you have been busy encouraging us to be community-minded, to help our neighbour, to reach out to strangers, to respect people of other faiths, or to care for God's creation - all very important matters. But perhaps some of you rarely mention Heaven's holiness and beauty, and the importance of penance and purification as well as prayer? Christ has asked me to offer a reminder that it is the task of priests today - as well as responsible parents, teachers and catechists - to tell the truth about those things which can seriously hamper our progress in prayer, and even prevent us from persevering in the Faith and reaching Heaven.

An invitation

Christ spoke with infinite tenderness to the woman **'who had been caught committing adultery'** (Jn 8:3), and to the crucified thief who said **'Jesus, remember me when you come into your kingdom'** (Lk 23:42). Yet the same Christ has warned us that **'anyone who does not carry his cross and come after me cannot be my disciple'** (Lk 14:27). That is why He has asked me to say to priests, today: It is certainly part of your duty to console and to encourage, as you so often do with gentleness and compassion. It is also part of your duty, however, to warn us about the attitudes and actions which can prevent us from making progress towards known union with God in prayer, and towards holiness and Eternal Life.

None of us must **'quench the wavering flame'** (Is. 42:3) through harshness or a lack of compassion; yet there are truths to be told about faith, about morals, and about reverence, for example, that some people are never going to hear unless we speak up. It might be our fault that they follow the 'broad way' I've illustrated, or fall off that ladder, because we have kept silent. These are the reasons why Christ has asked me to list a dozen of those dangerous attitudes and actions which are most common today.

He now asks you to look back, and to reflect upon the many homilies you have preached in past years. He asks you to think about the advice you've given to candidates or catechumens in RCIA classes, to parents who are preparing to have their baby baptised, to young people preparing for Confirmation, to young couples preparing for marriage, to young men preparing for the Priesthood, to sick people in danger of death, to Catholics in your care who tell you that they no longer believe in Catholic teaching on one matter or another, and to the Catholics you meet who no longer attend Mass.

The Faith, in its fullness

Christ asks you to consider these things: Have you worked consistently, by your words and example, to lead your people to believe and practice the Catholic Faith in its fullness, and to persevere in the Way marked out by Christ? How often have you preached on the following topics, and drawn your listeners away from a lukewarm attitude to God or a self-centred attitude to faith?

TWELVE SPIRITUAL DANGERS

1. Infrequent prayer

We are unlikely to persevere in the Faith if we rarely turn to God in prayer. How often do you remind your congregations that when we pray we are responding to the living God: the Majestic Creator of the whole Universe: God Who is so loving that He has **'leaned down from the heights of his sanctuary'** (Ps 102:19)? Have you told the people in your care that we have a duty to praise and thank Him daily, to ask for His help, and to intercede for other people? Have you warned those of us who rarely pray that we are endangering our souls?

Earthly friendships rarely last if one person cares so little for the other that he speaks only rarely, forgets special anniversaries, or can't be bothered to share news about special sadnesses or celebrations. The Lord is always reaching out to us, yet those of us who daily ignore Him, His Church, and His feast days need firm advice about keeping in touch with Him.

It is not essential for us to pray for long periods of time. Many people need reassuring that the Lord delights in our love for Him, even if we express that devotion in a mere five minutes of prayer each day - as well as in love for our neighbour. It is quality that 'counts' more than quantity, though there are great merits in different sorts of prolonged prayer. What is important for us all to learn is that only with the help of God, and the life of God in our souls, can we become happy 'children of God': gloriously alive, happy, pure and peaceful.

Through prayer, we can find the courage and strength to fight off the fiercest temptations, and to endure the lonely and heart-breaking 'desert' patches in our lives. Through regular, sincere, persevering prayer we can become more hopeful about reaching Heaven - there to see God face to face at last and to enjoy His love forever.

2. Refusing to accept unexpected suffering

It is easy for us to be distracted or made indignant by our pains and disappointments. Every priest knows of people who have resolved to follow Christ, but have later fallen away. They had an initial period of sweetness and joy, in the spiritual life, but were then surprised to meet unexpected sufferings. They became aggrieved or despairing, usually giving one of three reasons:

- 'I don't feel God's presence as I used to,' or
- 'Every time I pray, I feel guilty,' or
- 'How can I believe in a loving God, after this accident/illness/cruel treatment?'

Whenever newcomers approach the Church, today, they hear much cheerful news about the peace and fellowship that can be found at the heart of a loving community. Some are not warned, however, that we follow the way of the Cross. There are sufferings to bear, even if later we experience a spiritual resurrection. Without vigorous reminders from prayerful Catholics, newcomers might never learn that feelings of 'absence' or 'guilt' in prayer can be signs of God's closer presence. These can be invitations to look clearly at one's weaknesses, and to accept the forgiveness of God, Who loves us. And people who are taking the first steps on the Way sometimes forget that everyone on earth meets pain and disaster, at some stage. Is a follower of the crucified Christ to be exempt from ordinary mishaps and problems?

Every day, at Mass, you priests offer this astonishing prayer: ***'may we come to share in the divinity of Christ, who humbled himself to share in our humanity.'*** How often have you spoken about the sublime destiny to which we are called, and our need of perseverance - and purification? Have you ever explained the classic 'pattern' of Christian progress in prayer: through purgation and illumination to contemplation? You can open our eyes to the truth that by our sufferings, patiently accepted, we can grow in holiness, and help the Church, as I shall mention later on.

3. Self-centred instead of God-centred prayer

There is a wide-spread feeling today, about prayer, that we have failed if we don't 'enjoy' it.

Perhaps we have been led into prayer through an uplifting experience, such as sharing a happy retreat with friends. We have enjoyed the 'mood music', the candlelight, the perfumed oils, as well as the company. Yet if we keep trying to resurrect, at home, the sweet feelings we have enjoyed at the year's spiritual high points, there's a danger that our prayer will become self-centred rather than God-centred.

Have you encouraged us to turn to God in prayer whether our circumstances are pleasant or uncongenial and our minds tranquil or confused? Have you helped those who ask you for advice to see the truth about prayer? Truly, it is a conversation between a loving God and His own precious child. Yet we should not expect our prayer times to be a sort of spiritual holiday cruise: a journey with a vague Deity Who surely wants to make us 'feel good' at the end of a bad day.

No-one is as loving as our God; yet we cannot turn on His consolation as we turn on a tap, nor should we try. We should not mistake the sense of peace and contentment we find as we lie in an armchair listening to consoling music for the heights of spiritual union. The Lord is pleased when we enjoy the comforts He allows us; but known union with Him is achieved by those who persevere in prayer, out of love for Him, in every circumstance, even in personal weakness, persecution or disaster.

This is why Christ wants you to ask yourselves: Have you taught those of us in your care to pray to the Father in humility and gratitude, whatever our feelings? Have you taught us to approach the Father through Christ, in the Spirit, to offer daily praise and adoration as well as requests for help?

4. Lack of full attention in prayer

There is another great mistake about prayer, which we have all made, or been tempted to make. It is to believe so fervently that 'to work is to pray' that we give up the prayer of 'full attention' to God.

It is true that we please God when we are working, or helping others, for love of Him. Yet almost everyone, however busy, needs to find time to kneel once a day, even briefly, to pray to the Lord with whole-hearted attention. Sick persons, of course, will find other ways of praying. If we don't give our full attention to God, daily, it's because we don't choose to. We fail to make time for wholehearted intercession on behalf of others. Or we have not had the commonsense or the courtesy to make time to adore the Lord Who made us and Who invites us to meet Him in prayer, to enter His life and to be made holy.

Do you set a good example, in this matter? Do you spend time with the Lord, giving Him your full attention in times of personal prayer, and not just at Mass, in the Office, and praying with people in need? Have you explained and introduced Exposition of the Blessed Sacrament in your parish, with Adoration and Benediction - to encourage the quiet expressions of love for the Lord which complement those already offered during the Mass?

Have you explained to those you teach that when we open our hearts to God in silent attention, we allow Him to 'speak' to us? He has a thousand ways of speaking to us, both outside and inside prayer. But when we decide to pray, it's as if we choose to open the door of our hearts to Him. In our prayer, He might use words, or new insights, or images. He might implant good desires, to our surprise. He can wordlessly teach us how to praise Him. He can inspire feelings of awe, or gratitude. He can open our eyes to our sins and failings: not to scold us, but to enable us to make new resolutions, to ask for His help, and to change. Or He can 'hold' us in silence, as He trains us in trust and patience.

As a good mother trains her child in patience, whether before an exciting sports event or a visit to hospital, so the Lord needs to train us, at certain times. Yet how can He train us, or speak to us, if we are never told how important it is that we sometimes give Him our full attention and allow His Spirit 'free reign' within our souls?

5. *Clinging to our sins*

One of the reasons why many Catholics are reluctant to pray, and have little delight in the thought of Heaven, is that they cling to their sins. I am not speaking about our little faults. We all have faults. And we shall have faults and failings of one sort or another until we die, despite our efforts to change. I am speaking about serious sins. Some Catholics, who deliberately disobey God's laws or ignore the Church, act as if they have all the time in the world before they finally decide to lead good lives, and to make amends. It is really very important that you encourage us to have a right relationship with God now - if we will listen.

We know that God's love for us is constant and unshakeable, yet it is dangerous for us to cling to our sins, hoping that the Lord does not 'mind' if we follow our own inclinations, or supposing that there will be time to start again before we die. There are Catholics who refuse to attend Mass every week, for example, or who decide to marry 'outside' the Church. They may blithely tell us in conversation: 'How can we ruin the kids' Sunday?' - or 'How can God expect me to live alone, now that my marriage has broken up?'

Everyone with a kind heart will feel sympathy for others in their difficulties, yet those of us who deliberately disobey God and His Church will not make progress in prayer or in holiness until we have been helped to recognise and repent of our sins.

Christ asks you, His priests: Are you sharing the message found in Holy Scripture? *'We have been called by God to be holy, not to be immoral'* (1 Thess 4:7). Have you encouraged us to ponder, from time to time, whether we are doing all we can (by God's grace) to be *'judged worthy of a place in the other world and in the resurrection from the dead'* (Lk 20:35)? Do you actively encourage us all to change, or do you keep silent?

6. Over-emphasis on self-esteem

There is a praiseworthy desire today, in secular and religious circles, to make others feel valued and cherished. Yet that desire can become a determination never to make anyone 'feel bad'. We are thought most charitable, in some circles, if we refrain from speaking of right and wrong, offer only non-prescriptive counselling to unhappy people, and lavish only praise upon others, instead of warnings or truthful words about sin.

I have seen it suggested, in a teacher's manual for teenage Confirmation classes that no-one should ever be made to feel guilty by what the teacher says in class. Yet children need to be taught about sin and virtue. And which of us can hear about sin, without knowing ourselves to be guilty to some degree? We can cope with that knowledge, however, if we are also taught that God loves us in our weakness, and constantly offers His powerful graces, to help us to overcome our faults.

Christ asks you, His priests, to be simple, truthful and brave whenever you teach us about Christian behaviour. Though you might think that past presentations of the Catholic Faith have been overly-harsh and gloomy, you must not imitate those who attempt to redress the balance by offering a watered-down version. You cannot have failed to notice some of those programmes of instruction, whether for children or adults, which are seriously flawed in this respect.

In such programmes there is perhaps no mention of Original Sin or of our need of Redemption. You will find no mention of the importance of our remaining in a state of grace. Nothing is said about Satan and his attempts to draw us away from God. The explanations about self-worth are far longer than those about humility. You will find little mention of Christ's Cross, and how He died on it, sacrificing His life to save us from our sins. It is true that we are all precious in God's sight, and need to know it. Yet we need to recognise our indebtedness to Him, our continuing sinful inclinations, and the importance of growing in virtue, if we are to serve Him well, and be ready to enter Heaven when our work on earth is done.

Christ asks you not just to offer us consoling truths from the pulpit but to preach the Faith in its fullness. You can help us to grow in faith and humility if you teach us to look with awe and admiration upon God rather than upon ourselves.

It is a well-known adage that the Faith is 'caught not taught.' Though it is true that we cannot usually argue non-believers into belief, we can however clear up a few difficulties by sensible explanations. Similarly, although we cannot make young

Catholics practise the Faith by thrusting a Bible and a Catechism into their hands, we will neglect our duty if we suppose that Catholics learn about the Faith by a sort of spiritual osmosis and have no need of detailed instruction. We all need to be taught about God's plan of salvation, about how to control our sinful inclinations, how to practice the virtues - and what to do when we meet opposition or temptation.

7. Timidity

In encouraging people to become fervent, Spirit-led Christians, St. Paul wrote to the Corinthians: *'Be ambitious for the higher gifts'* (1 Cor 12:31). You priests are given great opportunities to help us to overcome the timidity that can hold us back from great work for God. You have all heard people say: "Oh, I could never be a Saint." Some people are secretly frightened by the thought of sacrifice. Others imagine that, for sanctity, one needs strong 'will-power' or great knowledge. They have so far remained unaware that the Saints are weak people who have said "Yes!" to God, and have allowed His Spirit to change and guide them. How marvellous it would be, if you could encourage us all to strive for sanctity just as earnestly as some people strive for perfect fitness or strive for excellence in various musical or social events.

We frequently see articles in our newspapers about people who are profoundly changed simply through reading a magazine article about creating a 'new self' by physical effort, new clothing, and a special diet. They are willing to run and sweat for hours, to fast, and to give away large sums of money, in order to be healthy and slim, and to attract a lot of attention. Yet these same people do not think it possible that with the same determination, and God's grace, they can achieve great sanctity, and achieve blissful union with God. By gentle but truthful explanations, you priests can help us to change our attitudes. Then we might allow the Lord to change our ambitions and goals. It needs to be said, however, that some faithful Catholics who might have been bold in proclaiming and defending the Faith have been made timid by comments heard from priests and religious.

Many of the laity, for example, feel helpless in sharing their faith because they have been made to feel 'old-fashioned' if they express concern about current sexual immorality. Or they are shocked when a missionary priest says he has no desire to convert people to the Faith. Or they are puzzled that their traditional devotions have been swept away. Or they are confused by the false versions of ecumenism practised so much today, and the indifferentism evident whenever faith in God is discussed. Or they retreat into silence when they hear their sincere Confessions dismissed as 'laundry lists'. Or they are astonished by the contrast between the sure teaching given by the Holy Father and some of the statements put out by their local Clergy or their representatives. Or they are dismayed by the sort of instruction some of their grand-children receive in Catholic schools. Or they wonder what to believe, when they attend Catholic conferences or retreats and are told by well-known speakers that the Church is mistaken in her long-held teachings.

The apparent timidity of these 'little ones' is the result of the Babel of contradictory voices heard in recent years. These timid Catholics deserve reassurance that the essentials of the Faith remain unchanged. They deserve to be told that even with the changes in discipline and attitudes which have been allowed by the Pope and the Bishops in communion with him, they are right to remain faithful to Christ and the Church, and to the well-established truths about faith and morals, and to share their faith as well as they can.

By a few reassuring words from the pulpit or in private conversation, you can encourage us to believe that we can achieve wonderful things for God. This might be in unseen work, rather than great projects. But you can remind those of us who are weak and fearful that we can love God and our neighbour with a strong, pure love, whatever our difficulties, because *'the love of God has been poured into our hearts by the Holy Spirit which has been given us'* (Rom 5:5).

If we trust in the power of the Spirit of God, try to discern His Will, and step out in faith wherever He leads us, we shall follow a sure Way. We shall meet all sorts of trials and hardships; but we shall do so in the company of our infinitely-loving Saviour. We shall find out one day, in extraordinary detail, how every sacrifice, every act of charity and every prayer has been worthwhile. This is what you can say about life in Christ: that He can bring us to the sort of fulfilment which is greater than anything we can imagine.

8. *Poor instruction*

Where Catholics have been poorly instructed there can develop a casual attitude towards the sacraments. Some people receive Holy Communion whatever the state of their souls. They never go to Confession. It would not occur to them to find someone to administer the sacrament of the sick to a dying relation. Some do not believe that by prayer and the sacraments we can be saved by Christ from sin and Hell, and made ready for Heaven. Some have grown cynical about the value of prayer to the Saints. Some have scarcely any devotion to Our Blessed Lady, who is seen as an 'optional extra' in their spiritual lives. Many no longer believe in the existence of the holy Angels. They show a similar disregard for the existence of the evil one, and his cohorts, who are at work to lead us away from faith and Christ. Some Catholics ignore the warnings of the Pope and the Bishops, and put their trust in New Age practices or unorthodox guides.

You priests are to be 'other Christs': truthful but tender towards the ignorant and sinful. Christ wants you to urge us to receive the sacraments, for the salvation of our souls. He wants you to tell us that the sacraments 'work'. They are powerful means of being in touch with God, and changed by God. We are wrong if we imagine that the sacraments are bits of cultural baggage that

Catholics must put up with, to please the older generation.

Christ asks you to put aside your fears about being unpopular. Speak, in appropriate language and at appropriate times, about sin and salvation, death and judgement, Heaven and Hell - and our need of God's graces. Speak about the peace and security to be found in a state of grace, knowing oneself to be a member of the 'Communion of Saints.' Try to ensure that we are well-instructed in faith and morals. If we allow ourselves to be influenced by the worldly opinions expressed all around us, we might end up losing all sense of sin. We shall slide away from the practise of the Faith and make little effort to keep the Commandments.

We need to be taught in detail the difference between right and wrong. We need to be assured that the Church has the authority from God to teach us, and to expect our obedience.

We read in the newspapers, daily, accounts of the wrongs perpetrated by people who have not had the benefit of sound teaching. Though their motives might be good, they neither honour God nor do good to others when they give out contraceptives even to children - or offer abortions to distressed women, or campaign for 'marriage' of persons in same-sex sexual relationships, or support legislation to allow the killing of sick and old people who are paralysed or in pain. You must remind us that although Christians might have a hard road to follow, it is the right road, revealed to us by Christ, Who wants us to lead us along it, all the way to Heaven.

St. Paul foretold such times as these when he wrote: *'far from being content with sound teaching, people will be avid for the latest novelty'* (2 Tim 4:3). You have a duty, as priests, to *'proclaim the message... welcome or unwelcome'* (2 Tim 4:1) - for the sake of the souls put into your care. The Lord will ask you, one day, what you did for us, to keep us on the Way to Heaven.

9. Disregard for the Magisterium.

There is plenty of evidence, in Catholic life today, of a dangerous disregard for the Magisterium, that is, for the teaching authority of the Pope and the Bishops in communion with him.

There are many Catholics who, whilst sincerely following their conscience, disagree with Church teaching. They have been urged to follow their consciences; yet they have not been told, with equal vigour, how dangerous it is to follow an erroneous conscience. They are not told how shocking it is that many a Catholic, today, is willing to stand up and say, in effect, "I know better than the Church. I know better than all the faithful Bishops, theologians, teachers and parents of the Church, of the past two thousand years. I know better than them what is right and wrong."

Do those Catholics say this from ignorance, or pride, or disbelief or confusion?

None of us can judge other peoples' hearts. But we do need to speak clearly about right and wrong and to say: It is very dangerous to differ from the Church on her constant teachings.

It is a cause for sadness, furthermore, that many of those Catholics who no longer believe in the Church's teachings on faith and morals unashamedly parade their disbelief. Some are proud of it. Some even attempt to persuade fellow-Catholics that we need no longer obey the long-held and authoritative teachings held out by the Pope and the other Catholic Bishops.

Christ asks, therefore: How many of you priests are pointing out the danger of elevating one's personal opinions above the constant teaching of the Church, for example, on matters such as the wrongness of contraception and abortion? Have you spent as much time explaining the need for chastity before marriage, and faithfulness within it, as you have speaking about the problems of poverty, arms sales and the environment? Have you made sure that the catechumens and candidates in your RCIA classes are receiving orthodox teaching on faith and morals? Have they been told about the obedience which Catholics should pay to the 'Ordinary' Magisterium, to the teachings of the Pope and the Bishops in communion with him, as explained in Lumen Gentium? Are they familiar not only with Holy Scripture, but also with the Catechism of the Catholic Church? Or is this succinct summary of Catholic doctrine left unused by those who want to offer a 'milder' version of the Faith?

Do you know what sort of text books and leaflets are being used in your catechetics classes? Have you read them? You are responsible for the souls in your care. Christ wants you to be as watchful about the written material selected by your Catechists for those they instruct as a good parent is about the reading matter offered by a school to his or her children. If you delegate, in the matter of handing on the Faith, you are still accountable to God for the quality of the teaching given by those to whom you have entrusted needy souls.

It is especially important that you promote Catholic teachings about marriage. These are constantly criticised even by catechists and teachers. They are criticised by some Catholic parents who have learned at first hand something of the pains and troubles of child birth and child care, and who want to avoid, even by sinful means, further pain, expense or inconvenience.

You priests do no favours to your flock if you suggest that the Church will change her teaching on marriage, chastity, and related topics. The constant teaching she offers in these matters is God's teaching: God's wishes expressed through the Church's teachers, the Bishops, even though they are frail human beings like all of us.

If you are brave, you will invite married people to live in accordance with the laws of God. We need to hear reminders that it is worthwhile to do so. We need assurances that we draw closer to God, and have a surer hope of Heaven, if we show our love for

God by doing His Will in every circumstance, whatever the cost.

If you are very brave you will ensure that you choose as catechists only those members of the Church who believe in the teachings of the Church. When a catechist decides that the Church is wrong in a long-standing teaching on faith or morals, and is not ashamed of her disbelief, but discusses it, she plainly no longer has a firm belief in related matters, such as the authority of the Pope who gives constant reminders of the Faith. She will be unable to teach the Faith with conviction, as she ought. She will teach a truncated or distorted version. Or she will describe the Faith in its fullness but with so many qualifications, and so many explanations which contrast the teaching of the 'official Church' with 'grass roots' opinions, that her listeners will develop the pick-and-mix approach to truth which is common today.

10. *Resentment*

There remain three major hindrances to progress in the spiritual life, which the Lord wants me to mention. These are resentment, grumbling, and irreverence. These three can even endanger our salvation, if we allow them to blossom and persist in our everyday lives. Yet they seem so harmless, like small weeds in a large garden.

Resentment is a poisonous weed which can kill every virtue it touches. It poisons our relationship with God, and with those around us. Those of us who give in to resentment might have the intention of being 'good Catholics', yet if we serve God with grudging hearts and sour faces, we are scarcely obeying the First Great Commandment of the Lord in a way worthy of 'children of God.'

We are all given powerful reminders today about the Second Great Commandment, which is to love our neighbour as ourself. There can be no-one who has missed an admirable exhortation to care for other people, especially the hungry, the disabled and the stranger in need. How often are we reminded, however, about our obligation to obey the First Great Commandment: ***'You must love the Lord your God with all your heart, with all your soul, and with all your mind'*** (Mt 22:37). How often do you priests urge us to show love for God not just by loving our neighbour but also by worshipping and adoring God at home and in church with grateful and reverent hearts?

Someone who prays to God with resentment and haste is like a mother who resents having to serve her family, and who routinely bangs the dishes onto the table at supper time. The Lord is not 'offended' by our carelessness, as a family might be offended by grudging service. Yet He sees that those who are full of resentment can hardly move closer to Him, whether they resent being required to bear the ordinary sufferings of life, or to fulfil their religious obligations.

11. *Incessant grumbling*

We have probably all been guilty of grumbling - about unexpected events, or painful disappointments. Yet by incessant grumbling we endanger our souls. If we constantly complain about the weather, or the Church, or our relations, or any other aspect of our daily lives, we cannot *'pray constantly'* (1 Thess 5:18). We do not have thankful hearts if we are constantly criticising God's Will for us, or giving in to self-pity.

We might make excuses for ourselves, saying, 'No-one has such dreadful pains as mine,' or 'No-one has to deal with such a difficult person, every day, all year.' But if we will not learn to control our grumbling, we will not have the thankful hearts which are a requirement for known union with God in prayer, and union with God in Heaven.

Some priests and other spiritual advisors tell us that since the Psalmist poured out his soul to God, in anger or confusion, we too can express our feelings to God without reserve. They are right, in that our trust in God should be absolute, even leading us to confide in Him about our worst failings and fears. He can help and heal us as no-one else can. Yet He is the living God, the all-holy One, Who deserves our trust, but not our impertinence, impatience and self-absorbed dissatisfaction.

We are impertinent and irreverent if we forget Who He is and who we are. He is all-loving, it is true. Yet He is all-pure and all-majestic, too. And though we should open our hearts to him, we ought not to grumble about His plans, like discontented servants. We need to train our minds, with His help, to see the good in every situation.

We also need help in seeing that our unavoidable sufferings, if accepted in patience, can be a means of joining in Christ's redeeming work and of helping the Church and the world.

12. *Lack of reverence*

Of the dozen failings which the Lord has asked me to mention today, one of the saddest to see is irreverence. We cannot look into some of our churches during a weekend Mass without seeing the evidence. Yet how many priests, Christ asks, are speaking the simple truth about the lack of respect currently shown for God in 'God's house.'

How many of you speak of the Lord with gladness and conviction, sharing the good news that He is real, He is beautiful, He is overflowing with love, and is so loveable that He deserves the best we can give Him: the best service, and the best respect?

If you don't teach us, some of us will never know how good He is - nor how majestic and glorious, infinitely powerful as well as infinitely kind. Nor will we realise what respect and reverence is due to Him in His own 'house of prayer' where Christ the Son of God is sacramentally Present in the tabernacle.

If you don't speak to people about how to behave in church, some will never realise that we should behave in church in a way which is different from the way we behave in a Burger Bar or a Sports Centre.

No kind priest wants to cause hurt or embarrassment by needless criticism of those he serves. And priests are very aware, for example, of the difficulties parents have with their babies and young children. Each priest needs to question his own motives, however, when he refrains from giving reminders about appropriate behaviour in church. Perhaps fear, or an anxiety to 'keep the peace,' stop him speaking out. But it is not charitable for the priest to say nothing whilst the people in his care:

- habitually arrive late for services,
- never genuflect on entering their places in the church,
- attend Mass wearing immodest clothing,
- as Eucharistic Ministers, wear immodest or ostentatious clothing,
- promote so-called 'liturgical dancing' by girls and women in scanty garments,
- allow children to run riot,
- chatter loudly before, during, or immediately after the Mass, thus disturbing those who pray, and showing little respect for Christ Who is Really Present in the tabernacle,
- forget the presence, besides us, in our churches, of the holy Angels.

The irreverent behaviour I've had to describe needs to be corrected for two main reasons. First, it is insulting to the Lord. He does not take offence; yet He does not deserve such disrespect. But secondly, our irreverence has a harmful effect on us.

If we are careless and irreverent in the presence of our Heavenly King we are unlikely to achieve the joy the Lord wants to share with us, in prayer and in Eternity. Christ asks you, His priests, to help us to overcome our ignorance and laziness. You can remind us to behave as loving and reverent *'children of God'* (Rom 8:16) when we cross the 'threshold' of our church and stand before Christ on the brink of Heaven. You can help in different ways, and not only by offering reminders about behaviour. If you teach the truth about the Holy Sacrifice of the Mass you will bring some of your flock to their knees before God in gratitude and wonder.

How many of the people in your care know that the Mass is more than a family meal for Catholics? How often have you reminded us that at every Mass we are in the presence of the God-man Who suffered for our sins and Who, out of love for us, died to make us holy?

How often have you explained that the Mass is primarily a re-presentation of the once-for-all sacrifice of Christ? How many of us know that at every Mass it's as if we are at the foot of the Cross, with Mary? (C.C.C. para. 1370). Christ has arranged that since we could not be present, long ago, as He carried out His saving work, we can be present at Mass, where the very sacrifice once offered by Christ on Calvary is re-presented on our altar, though in a different, sacramental manner. How many Catholics know this?

How many Catholics know that we receive not ordinary bread in Holy Communion, but Christ Himself, the 'Holy One,' Who is truly and substantially Present amongst us? How many Catholics realise that the sacred meal we share is a communion with Christ our God Who has redeemed us by His sacrifice?

Have you ever reminded us that if we are living in serious sin, we ought to go to Confession before next receiving Holy Communion?

No conscientious mother fails to teach her children good manners. No responsible adult takes visitors to a civic award ceremony or any formal celebration without explaining what sort of behaviour is expected of the participants. In Christ's sight, all priests involved in pastoral work have a duty to remind us about the meaning of the Mass, and to encourage us in reverent and respectful behaviour.

We give more glory to God, and achieve greater holiness if, in meeting together to offer the Holy Sacrifice, we show out some degree of gratitude and awe in God's presence.

You can also encourage us to approach God, in our prayers at home, with a greater humility. An extraordinary number of Catholics who have admirably persevered in daily prayer at home nevertheless describe how they lie in bed to recite their prayers. Or they settle in an armchair at each prayertime, to unwind with some mood-music.

There is nothing wrong with praying to God whilst we are in bed, or snug in an armchair. On the contrary, He is always pleased when we open our hearts to Him, whatever our circumstances. But something has gone wrong in our thinking if these ways are the only ways in which we 'meet' God in our homes.

How are we showing tremendous reverence towards God our Father, in admiration and humble praise, if we cannot occasionally be bothered to kneel before Him, as Christ did, and the Apostles? Have the Saints throughout the ages all been wrong, in their tremendously reverent approach to God, and in the acts of humility and penance they offered to God in their daily prayer?

It is true that prayer at home can be made extra difficult today, where many families no longer pray together, or where only one of the spouses is a Catholic, or only one is Christian. It can be difficult to find a place in which to kneel and pray in busy households or cramped quarters. Someone who lies in bed to pray might deserve praise for his faithfulness rather than queries about his attitudes. We must *'never pass judgement on a brother or treat him with contempt'* (Rom 14:10). Yet our prayer life will develop more swiftly if we are determined to show God that we realise that He is all-holy as well as all-compassionate. We can do this by our reverent posture as well as through our thoughts.

You priests can remind us that the Saints have not grown close to God in prayer by doing 'the minimum'. Without fervent and reverent prayer they would never have been successful in their family life, or their preaching, or their missionary work, or their God-inspired ways of bringing help to the poor. Nor would they have achieved blissful, known union with God in the God-given prayer of contemplation.

A generation has been taught about God's love for each of us. But there is a great need for clear instruction on the holiness and purity of God. We need to act with reverence towards Him, and to grow in His likeness, if we are to find contentment in His service on earth and joy in His presence in Heaven.

While I'm on the subject of respect and reverence, it's important to say that the Lord wants us, the laity, to have a proper respect for you, and for your vocation as Catholic priests.

It's plain that very few of you act as *'dictators'* (2 Cor 1:24) over us. By your faithful service most of you inadvertently give us daily lessons in humility and charity. But you must never allow yourselves to be made despondent if we fail to treat you with the respect you deserve. Whether we do so from weakness, ignorance, or malice, you can be sure that the Lord holds you in great esteem. He cares very deeply about you, and wants you to confide in Him about every aspect of your lives - which should include your hurts and disappointments as well as your causes for gratitude and joy.

I once spoke flippantly to a priest about an aspect of his priestly duties - then regretted what I had said. Indeed, next time I prayed, I saw the Lord before me. He was looking towards me, gently but solemnly saying to me: 'My priests are sacred.' That gentle statement told me, more powerfully than any obvious rebuke, how important it is in Christ's sight that we lay-persons give you a special respect because you represent Christ, for us, in our local communities.

Perhaps this will make you realise, anew, that if you yourselves speak flippantly about your Priesthood or your sacred duties, you set a bad example and demean your privileged state. If, however, by the grace of God, you have a loving and Christ-like demeanour, if you always act with dignity and patience, if you speak and work with neither haste nor irritation, and if you avoid all worldly or vulgar chatter and gossip, you will help us to see Christ in you. You will allow His Spirit to shine out from your heart and soul; and your ministry will be genuinely Christ-like and fruitful.

READY FOR HEAVEN?

The top of the ladder

Now that I've listed the twelve spiritual dangers - those particular attitudes or actions by which we hamper our spiritual progress - it's time to return to the images which Christ has given me.

Christ asks you to look again at that narrow ladder which each of us must climb, if we are to persevere on our journey to Heaven. Climbing the ladder, remember, represents our perseverance in faith. In picture *3: 'With bleeding hands,'* I reproduce what Christ has shown me about someone who has almost reached Heaven. That person clings with bloodied hands onto the higher rungs, weary with the effort both to hold on, and to resist the attacks of the evil one who hovers nearby.

This brave soul is at that stage of the spiritual life where he has lost the joy experienced at his long-ago conversion. He feels little joy at the thought of Heaven. Yet with all his power he keeps climbing in the darkness, even when shaken by fear at the assaults of the evil one and thoughts of his own weakness. He relies on the grace of Christ for endurance, since Heaven is not yet in sight. Yet such torment does not last forever.

Christ cannot leave His friends feeling desolate forever. Picture *4: 'Waiting to greet us,'* shows the top of the ladder, where the darkness is replaced by glory. This newly-arrived soul will not remain alone, exhausted, unsure whether the difficult times are really over. The bright cloud which he encounters represents the Godhead. There, at the 'edge' of Heaven, Christ and Our Lady are waiting to greet each newcomer. They are full of delight whenever another faithful soul arrives to share their joy and glory.

Although many faithful souls will need further purification, each will be led, eventually, into in **'the city of the living God, the heavenly Jerusalem where the millions of angels have gathered for the festival'** (Heb 12:22). Amidst clouds of glory, each soul is met with great tenderness and love, and assured of salvation.

The Holy Trinity

This is our destiny, if we accept it: to share with all the Saints and holy Angels in the life of the Holy Trinity for all Eternity, in bliss and glory. A further image which Christ has given me - not reproduced here - shows something of that glory as seen from within Heaven; indeed, from the 'heights' of Heaven. And from within all that glory can be seen, far off, the tiny globe of the earth, and the 'ladder' by which the Saints have made their way to Heaven.

From this perspective, the ladder is foreshortened. Earthly life and its trials seem to be very brief, when set beside the magnificence and bliss found in Eternal Life, where there is no danger of loss, or sadness or pain. And this is the perspective that Christ asks you to keep in mind, as you do your priestly work.

Christ wants you to be able to say, with St. Paul: *'I believe nothing can happen that will outweigh the supreme advantage of knowing Christ Jesus my Lord. For him I have accepted the loss of everything, and I look on everything as so much rubbish if only I can have Christ and be given a place in him'* (Phil 3:8-9). If you can say these words from your heart, you will have no hesitation in urging us, whom you teach and advise, to give Christ first place in our lives, and to prepare for life with Him in Heaven.

A SPECIAL MESSAGE

The Christ-child

When I had written out, a few weeks ago, the long list of reminders that Christ asked me to share with you for the sake of the people in your care, I wondered how I should end my talk. I longed to end on a hopeful note. I wondered if Christ had some special encouragement for you, in your often-lonely work. So I was pleased, though surprised, when He suddenly put before me an image which I had just painted for my Christmas card this year: *5: 'The Christ-child.'* This is a simple image of an innocent child, in swaddling clothes, who holds out His little arms towards us.

It is true that, as priests, you have seen hundreds of nativity scenes, and hundreds of Christ-childs. Perhaps we all take such images for granted. Nevertheless, Christ has asked me to offer you this painting of Himself as a little child, with a special message for you who are 'other Christs' amongst us. There are three points He asks you to reflect upon:

- Christ asks you to consider once more the humility and trust He showed as He began His life on earth as God made man.

- Christ asks you to persevere in humility and trust as you continue, today, your share of His important work.

- Christ asks you to do so even in poor circumstances, even amidst your personal weaknesses, and even though you might be surrounded by people who believe that you are wasting your time or who offer you only gloomy opinions about the future of the Church.

The Catholic Church will endure to the end of time. There will be wonderful 'flowerings' of faith in unexpected places, and new Saints will arise to inspire and encourage us. Some of you might be amongst them. Christ asks you to persevere in love, and in faithfulness. Through your preaching you can encourage us to persevere. Through your offering of the Holy Sacrifice, you enable us to 'touch' Heaven. It is through your ministry that we in the Church, together, daily, can offer worthy praise to the Father, through Christ, in the Spirit. We can offer worthy thanks for all that is good. We can offer reparation for our sins; and we can ask with great confidence for the Father's help, because we ask with and through Christ our Saviour.

Christ looks on with gratitude and joy as you determine, day after day, to fulfil your priestly duties. And that same Christ whose Sacrifice you offer daily, to the glory of the Father, has asked me to offer you this booklet, to encourage you to be brave and childlike and prayerful in His service.

Further illustrations

You can find other paintings reproduced in this little book, all of them given to me by Christ. These other images were gifts from

Him in earlier years; but they illustrate some of the important things mentioned in the text, and so perhaps they will prove useful.

CONCLUSION

Your vocation

Christ asks each of you to *'proclaim the message and, welcome or unwelcome, insist on it. Refute falsehood, correct error, call to obedience'* (1 Ti 4:1). In this way, you can help the Catholics in your care, and show the Way of Christ to some of the *'sheep without a shepherd'* (Mt 9:36) in your area. Then you will be more likely to have a peaceful conscience in the presence of Christ, when you meet Him face to face in Eternity, and when you reflect, in His presence, on how well you have fulfilled your vocation.

Each of you priests can assure one another, speaking about Christ: *'Through him we received grace and our apostolic mission to preach the obedience of faith to all pagan nations in honour of his name'* (Rom 1:5). If you remain faithful to the end you will be glad that you have been brave enough to *'warn the idlers, give courage to those who are apprehensive, care for the weak and be patient with everyone.'* (1 Thess 5:14). You will be overwhelmed with joy that Christ has allowed you to do His work on earth and to save souls, bringing people who were once blind or hopeless *'out of the darkness into his wonderful light'* (1 Pet 2:9).

* * * * * * *

1. A dark world

There was a vast gulf between earth and Heaven, caused by sin. That gulf was bridged by Jesus Christ the Son of God, Who was made man and lived amongst us.

2. The ladder to Heaven

Christ has given us a narrow way to Heaven so we can share in the glory of the Saints - even if we first need to be purified in Purgatory. There is a 'broad road' to Hell, that we can follow if we choose.

3. With bleeding hands

The Christian will experience times of darkness and isolation, of spiritual assaults and earthly persecution. We need to persevere in faithfulness to Christ just as determinedly as someone who clings to a rope-ladder even with bleeding hands.

4. Waiting to greet us

Our earthly trials cannot last forever. Christ and His Mother Mary are waiting to greet us, as if at the 'edge' of Heaven, when our work for Him on earth is finally done.

5. The Christ-child

The infant Jesus can be our model, as we ponder the lowliness and weakness He chose to experience, for our sakes. Christ asks us to live in humility and trust as we undertake our share of His saving work - even in our weakness.

6. Preaching to wounded souls

Many people are vulnerable and fragile. The Great Physician asks His priests to heal us through their truthful words and loving administration of the sacraments.

7. A warning is an act of charity

Here we see a loving person speaking to a friend about the danger that friend is in because of the overhang on which he stands to admire the view. We too act with charity whenever we speak the truth, with respect and love, to warn those we know who endanger their souls by their sinful moral choices.

8. Out of communion

Someone saws through the branch of a tree on which he and his friends are perched. The inevitable fall will be disastrous for them all. In the tree trunk are embedded images of the Pope and Bishops, and of the Faithful. This picture hints at the dreadful consequences of deliberately walking away from the Catholic Church.

9. The Institution of the Eucharist

Here we see the once-for-all saving Sacrifice of Christ, which was anticipated by Him at the Last Supper, then offered from the Cross on Calvary, and which is now offered from our altar through the ministry of the priest.

10. Christ our Intercessor

A huge, radiant Christ stands before the altar at Mass. A priest stands behind the altar, holding up the Sacred Host, echoing the gesture of Christ Who prays to the invisible Father, in the Spirit. Mighty flames represent both Christ's Divinity and the presence of the Holy Spirit. At every Mass we offer Christ's Sacrifice, and Christ's praise and thanks, to our Heavenly Father.

A final passage from St. Paul's Letter to the Ephesians.

'Grow strong in the Lord, with the strength of his power. Put God's armour on so as to be able to resist the devil's tactics. For it is not against human enemies that we have to struggle, but against the Sovereignties and the Powers who originate the darkness in this world, the spiritual army of evil in the heavens. That is why you must rely on God's armour, or you will not be able to put up any resistance when the worst happens, or have enough resources to hold your ground.

So stand your ground, with truth buckled round your waist, and integrity for a breastplate, wearing for shoes on your feet the eagerness to spread the gospel of peace and always carrying the shield of faith so that you can use it to put out the burning arrows of the evil one. And then you must accept salvation from God to be your helmet and receive the word of God from the Spirit to use as a sword.

Pray all the time, asking for what you need, praying in the Spirit on every possible occasion. Never get tired of staying awake to pray for all the saints; and pray for me to be given an opportunity to open my mouth and speak without fear and give out the mystery of the gospel of which I am an ambassador in chains; pray that in proclaiming it I may speak as boldly as I ought to.' (Eph 6:10-20)

What is Radiant Light?

Radiant Light is a Movement within the Roman Catholic Church. It seeks to encourage people to grow in holiness by believing and living the Catholic faith in its fullness. It was founded by Elizabeth Wang, at the request of Christ, and its mission is inspired by the teachings, images, and spirituality which He has given her in prayer. Christ is 'the radiant light of God's glory' (Heb 1:3).

Please write to the Harpenden address below if you would like to be put on the Radiant Light mailing list.

If you would like to help support the work of Radiant Light, please send a UK cheque to **Radiant Light, 25 Rothamsted Avenue, Harpenden, Herts, AL5 2DN, U.K.** Cheques must be made payable to 'Radiant Light'. Thank you.

Company No. 3701357 (Company limited by guarantee and not having a share capital).

For information about other publications or about how to purchase Radiant Light products please visit the Radiant Light web-site at:
www.radiantlight.org.uk